BLAZING YOUR PATH
THROUGH LIFE

Blazing Your Path Through Life

How to Turn Your Personal Potential Into Results

Jim Zwers

Prominent Books

Writing: Jim Zwers
Editing & Layout: Writer Services, LLC

ISBN 10: 1942389051
ISBN 13: 978-1-942389-05-7

ACKNOWLEDGMENTS

This book is dedicated to all the people who inspire me to be better than I am and who work so hard to make the world around us a better place.

Specifically, I'd like to thank the young people I work with who share so much of their wonder and energy with me every day.

I'd like to thank my fellow educators who dedicate their lives to the most noble goal of making the next generation the best that they can be.

Lastly, I want to thank my family who has supported me and loved me and given me the confidence to dream big.

ABOUT THE PHOTOGRAPHS IN THIS BOOK

All photos were taken by myself on my various travels. I added ones that I felt expressed some of the beauty I've witnessed around the world.

—Jim Zwers

TABLE OF CONTENTS

Prologue ix

Introduction 1

1. The Quality of Leadership 7

2. Nature vs. Nurture 13

3. The Power of One's Decisions 21

4. The Key to Genius 27

5. On Mediocrity, Greatness, Dreams and Courage 35

6. Luck and the Future 45

7. Five Gifts from My Mother 55

8. Choices 67

9. The Future 77

Conclusion 83

About the Author 85

Prologue

Transitions

In life, we are in a repeating cycle of working toward an objective, and then transitioning toward the next objective. Working, transitioning, working, transitioning. Graduation is just one of many such transitions in life: starting school, graduating, moving to a new city, getting married, changing careers, seeing our own children go off to college. At any one of these points of transition there are decisions to be made, goals to be set, things to say goodbye to and new people and places to discover.

Sometimes the transition comes on its own, and sometimes we shake things up by instigating our own changes in our lives. Sometimes we see the transition coming from far away and other times they happen, out of the blue, completely unexpected.

Who is This Book For?

In putting these speeches together in book form, I realized that in addition to the obvious fact of these applying directly to a graduating student, they could also be useful to anyone going through any period of change in his or her life, whether planned or unexpected.

There are times that we all have to make decisions, to make changes. I hope this book helps readers to make tough decisions and make them better.

ABOUT MAKING DECISIONS

As a quick note of importance, just because you made a wrong decision in the past or failed at some goal doesn't mean that the game is over for you. Making the wrong decision might just be a step you had to go through to get to the ultimate right place.

The hardest part of this process of writing a book has been getting over the feeling that someone would think that I think I have all the answers to life. I don't. But I have found everything in these pages to be relevant and useful in my own life. I work hard to learn more and become better every day and to that degree practice what I preach in this book.

Good luck and fair weather as you move through the adventures of your life.

—Jim Zwers

INTRODUCTION

THE ECONOMICS OF ADVICE

In economics, there is a concept known as supply and demand. It determines how much something is worth. For example, if there is a short supply of something (take gold for instance), it becomes more valuable in the eyes of the consumer. Likewise, if there is a high demand for something, the price rises.

The opposite of this is when there is low demand or too much of something. In this case the value drops and so does its price.

Most advice is ignored for two reasons: 1) the advice-giver thinks he is smarter than you, which is a complete turnoff and makes you not want to listen, or 2) the advice-giver wants you to avoid the mistakes he's made in the past, which makes him, by default, seem dumber than you. Either way, it's a deal-breaker with no interest in listening to the knowledge that person has to share.

This creates an economic condition where there is a lot of advice available, but there's very little demand for it. In fact, there is so little demand for advice that it creates an inverted condition whereby the one receiving any advice is just "listening" to be nice to the person who's giving the advice. Economically, it is a negative demand!

It's to the point where people who are willing to sit and listen to another's advice are so rare, you could almost be paid to do so.

Anyway, back to my point. I want to share information with you but I want to avoid giving you advice (which you don't really want anyway). So, for the next few pages let's just imagine that we're just friends having a conversation.

WHY I WROTE THIS BOOK

We begin our lives with curiosity, opposition and determination, among other things. At first, decisions are made for us almost completely. The older we get, the more the tide turns to our own control. That control, self-appointed or otherwise, is in the area of responsibility. It has nothing to do with going it alone, figuring it all out and doing things all by yourself.

We can move along by guessing—taking best chances—and hoping things turn out like we want them to. Though trying something is better than "playing it safe" and doing nothing, to approach goals with no knowledge of the path, a lot of time, energy and finance can be needlessly wasted.

There are a great many things to accomplish, so approaching things with less guesswork will allow for more success much sooner. This can be done by at least considering the advice of others whom you trust, who have shown success in the areas that you intend to adventure into.

A road taken with a decent map, out of the previous experience of others, showing the potholes, dead ends, speed traps and treacherous cliffs will be faster and further traveled. If you've ever wondered why some people are better at something than others, rest assured, they have listened to good coaches along the way.

Doing something by yourself may be a feat well-deserving of praise. But it is a wise person who is willing to listen to knowledge and experience of others

Once in a while, a teacher, an elder or possibly even a fictitious hero will say something that, to us, is meaningful. It causes a light to shine brighter within us. Our whole basis of how we think, behave and do things can be greatly influenced.

Over the years, I've delivered speeches as the Executive Director at Clearwater Academy International to the graduating classes. These addresses were given in hope of creating a positive influence, encouragement and perhaps shed some wisdom from my own experiences.

But how does someone send off a group of young women and men so they have ample advice to kickstart things, within such a limited allocation of time of maybe fifteen minutes, all the while hoping that something really sinks in and stays with them in their journeys? And what about the years prior and past that could possibly make a positive impact upon their decisions, actions and lives in general as well?

Each year, I saw new things to talk about that our past classes wouldn't get the chance to hear. I too was still learning about people and life and so on. And after fourteen years, I can say with humility that there is information worth sharing, worth contemplating, that can positively influence, if only from lessons learned and achievements made—whether stumbled upon or deliberately thought out. This, for the most part, was the impetus for this book.

The following pages are a compilation of my graduation speeches for the past nine years with even further thoughts and illumination upon their messages. It is not intended to be read cover-to-cover, but rather absorbed and thought about a little at a time.

This book was made to help young people and adults jump-start their lives. Its purpose is to fuel your flame with insightful ideas.

I hope you will be encouraged, inspired and unstoppable with the great things you want to accomplish. You should certainly walk away knowing that life is an active game, and you can play to win with what I share.

To Life!

However, "Leadership" is a quality we can have in us regardless of what our position in the group is. It's a quality we can have within us like honesty, courage, or compassion.

1. THE QUALITY OF LEADERSHIP

COMMENTARY

The quality of leadership is something that affects all of our lives directly and indirectly. Leadership as a quality doesn't only involve telling others what to do and getting them to follow one, but it concerns taking the path that is right regardless of whether or not anyone is following at all.

A true leader does what is right in tough circumstances and isn't concerned about status or accolades. The world needs more leaders – not just to tell others what to do but to set the trail and guide society toward a higher state. There are many out there pushing society in certain directions for their own benefits. A true leader pushes society for the benefit of others.

COMMENCEMENT ADDRESS 1

Thank you, everyone, for coming out tonight to honor the hard work and accomplishments of our students.

You know, it is almost a cliché with private schools that, "We are making the leaders of tomorrow." You see it on websites and promo and printed on letterhead. I always smile to myself and wonder, do these schools have football teams with eleven quarterbacks? Or do they only have presidents on their student council?

Being a leader is important, but I've always sort of felt that it isn't really the correct statement of what we are trying to accomplish in a school. What if someone wants to be a really good mother? Does this mean she isn't a product of the school if she isn't the head of the PTA or in *The Guinness Book of World Records* for the most babies? What about a writer? If they aren't writing best-selling novels, have they failed?

Sometimes we take the easy way out and say, "Well, as long as I'm happy, that's all I care about." Just chasing happiness, though, isn't enough. True happiness itself is really just the reward for doing the right things and accomplishing one's goals.

So I looked at the concept of leadership and realized that true leadership isn't just telling others what to do but is taking responsibility for the direction of the group and the accomplishment of its goals. This responsibility can happen from any position in an organization.

You see, being a leader is often thought of as a position, like being team captain: calling the shots and making decisions. However, "Leadership" is a quality we can have in us regardless of what our position in the group is. It's a quality we can have within us like honesty, courage or compassion.

In this sense I believe that this school does promote and graduate young men and women who have that special quality and look in their eye, that they can and will take responsibility for their area, that they have Leadership.

In fact our system is built to do just that. Our students are given the responsibility for their education right from the start and in order to graduate, they really have to embrace that responsibility.

In contrast to this, in most schools there is a certain laziness that sets in at the end of high school. They even have a name for it – it's called "Senioritis." However, our students typically become more productive and work harder as they near graduation.

The ability to overcome challenges is an important quality and I think it is one that each of our graduates share tonight. Some have overcome language barriers, study difficulties, and even those who were good students, challenged themselves by working harder, taking more difficult classes or setting tough goals to graduate early.

Confronting and dealing with obstacles is a big part of leadership and something our graduates have all demonstrated.

Our school isn't designed to give everyone the exact same education since our philosophy is based on a very individual viewpoint of every student. We call it Goals Oriented Education and you see it in our graduates.

And to this graduating class I say: You've worked hard and gotten one of the best educations available. I don't think that any of you believes that this is the end of all learning, but it is an important milestone and one you can always look back on with pride and the knowledge that you are a graduate of Clearwater Academy.

In closing, I have one last lesson for you before you leave. It's a piece of advice that was given to me at summer camp when I was growing up.

It's the line, "You get out of life what you put into it." The camp counselors used to preach this to us regularly and we used to just roll our eyes. At the time, we used to think it was just a trick to get us to participate more in activities – those sneaky camp counselors. I didn't realize the truth of it until much later.

"You get out of life what you put into it."

For some reason, the line stuck with me and I began to see more and more how it was true. When you're involved in life, active and engaged, you do get more out of it. Life is more exciting and dramatic and interesting when you're involved.

"You get out of life what you put into it."

So for you graduates, my hope is that you take on life with your full energy. Don't be timid; take risks; fall in love; take the harder road sometimes and be sure to stop in from time to time and let us know how you're doing.

You will always be a part of this school and we hope we have become an unforgettable part of your lives. And sometime in the future when things seem difficult or impossible, when you've taken on too much or life seems to be going against you, think back to this night and realize you've done something great and you are special.

Some people wait around their whole life, waiting for their big break, hoping for something good to happen to them rather than making it happen.

2. NATURE VS. NURTURE

COMMENTARY

How much we are the product of our environment and how much we bend our environment to our advantage is an important area of thought. It can sometimes seem that the whole world is against us and life just favors others more and they have all the luck.

Regardless of factors of "luck" there is so much we can control and take advantage of in life. If we live life fully and make the most of the opportunities we have, each of us is capable of so much more.

Living life is a busy activity. It requires getting what we want sometimes but also working and cooperating with others. Together, anything can be accomplished; alone, only the work of a single person is possible.

COMMENCEMENT ADDRESS 2

Tonight, rather than give you a speech, I'd like to read you a fairy tale. After all, isn't that how most of your educations started out, with fairy tales? It's only fitting that it should end with one.

(Open book)

Once upon a time, before the Internet and before cell phones and before you were even born, there existed a magical time. That time was called the 80's.

It was a special time when women wore shoulder pads like football players, rock bands had hair past their shoulders and your parents were actually cool.

During this time there was a movie called *Trading Places*. It starred Dan Aykroyd and Eddie Murphy. In the magical time of the 80's, both of these actors made really funny movies.

In this movie, Dan Aykroyd was the successful result of going to all the right schools, knowing the right people and using the right connections.

Eddie Murphy was the exact opposite: a street-wise troublemaker, scraping just to get by.

Near the beginning of the movie, two old men are talking and debating whether Nature or Nurture was the determining factor in a person's success.

Nature vs. Nurture is an idea which asks whether a person is successful because of his environment and upbringing (how he is nurtured, meaning cared for) or whether the person's nature, his natural abilities in life, determines his success.

You get this concept: it's natural ability versus the environment around the person.

Most parents know of these ideas instinctively. For example: when you're doing well, it's because of their superior parenting skills and when you're not doing well, it's because of your bad, bad nature.

Back to our story ...

The two old men decide to test out this theory and make a bet to see which one is right. They then proceed to change the lives of our stars to show how, by changing their surroundings and changing factors in their environment, they can make Dan Aykroyd a failure and Eddie Murphy successful.

They do a lot of things to make this happen and throughout most of the movie you see Dan getting worse and worse, and Eddie getting better and better. Finally, Dan is a beaten man and Eddie is wildly successful. The first old man has proven his side of the argument and won the bet. He proved that one's environment formed and changed the lives of our stars. Bad old man.

But wait! The story doesn't end there. You see, Eddie and Dan figure out what is going on and set out to create their own plan to get back at the two bad men. Yay! Revenge!

They then do a bunch of stuff and the old men lose a bunch of money and our stars get a bunch of money and the movie has a happy ending.

A lot of movies in the 80's had to do with people getting a lot of money. Money was important at that time, not like now when no one cares about money.

So maybe you're sitting there wondering, "So what's the point? Yeah, Mr. Zwers, what is the point? Did nature beat nurture? Why are we talking about this? When do I get my diploma?"

Well, this is a fairy tale, and as we all know, fairy tales usually have a lesson. So what is the message of this story? Is it that you are supposed to avoid old people? Is it that nature beats nurture? Is it that money is good?

No, my friends, the lesson of this story is that when you are the star of the movie, things always work out for you in the end.

And that is what I hope for each of you. In many ways your life, until now, has been a rehearsal and now it's showtime. We've done what we could to teach you and inspire you. Now it's time to take the leading role in the story of your own life!

Many people go through life as a minor character in their own lives, timid, worried what others will think of them, being afraid to take charge, always following another's wishes, ignoring their own hopes and dreams. These people take minor roles, being more interested in the lives of others than their own.

Maybe this is somehow linked to reality TV, watching other people live their lives rather than living our own. Watching others' lives and wishing that they were our own, or happy that they aren't our lives, but we're still watching.

Watching rather than living. It's not just related to TV or video games. Some people wait around their whole lives waiting for their big break, hoping for something good to happen to them rather than making it happen.

But on the other hand, let me give you some examples of the advantages of being the star:

- Bullets don't hit you when you're shot at, and even if they do, it's usually just a flesh wound.
- The star gets the girl (or boy).

16

- Stars drive cooler cars.
- Best of all, the star is still there in the final scene of the movie.

Now, I'm not suggesting you all run around frantically trying to gain everyone's attention. Just lead your life, don't let life lead you.

So for you, my hope is that you take on the starring roles in your lives—your big, big lives. We've done what we could to teach you, to give you meaningful experiences and to help as needed. Now it's up to you.

(Look at book)

And the graduating class lived exciting lives ever after.

(Close book)

The End.

What I'm talking about is *actually* making things different because of one's outlook.

3. The Power of One's Decisions

Commentary

Beyond your family and ring of close friends, there's a world out there that's steeped in social attitude that has become sort of "reluctantly accepting" of "the way things are."

It's pretty much expected that any light conversation between strangers will be about how bad things have been, how the government or spouse or some other thing is at fault for things not going their way.

It's easy to slip into bad habits, especially when they're habits of the way we think. Daily chants, which are no more than negative complaints, become reality.

It's all rather vague, but can be very convincing when you hear the negativity enough times. You might even find yourself starting or joining in on conversations that way after a while, if you don't remain aware of its destructive nature.

For each one of us, the world is ours to approach and deal with as we see fit. That, by itself, enables you to say exactly how things are for you. And this all begins with your personal attitude.

Just as the "habitual negative attitudes" shared so openly by others can be contagious, so too can your positive outlook (which is the only way to go) help raise up everyone around you, not to mention keep your attitude in the right place. If you go through life with you deciding how to think and feel about things, you will accomplish a lot of great things for yourself, and others.

COMMENCEMENT ADDRESS 3

I have a final gift for the graduating class.

My gift is a gift of wisdom. (I'm sorry, but you should have seen this coming.)

Some 2000 years ago, Gautama Siddhartha Buddha, the founder of Buddhism, said: "All that we are is the result of what we have thought: it is founded on our thoughts, it is made up of our thoughts."

This is amazing when you think about it. It means that everything you are, everything you have, everything you do, starts with thought.

These thoughts can be decisions: decisions to like something, decisions to hate something; decisions to do something, decisions not to do something. It includes our hopes and dreams. All these are the thoughts which shape our lives.

I think we've all known people who have a negative outlook on life, and when bad things happen to them it just proves to them that their outlook was justified. People are always trying to do them in, life is rigged against them.

Others have a more positive outlook and things work out for them as they expect—in a positive way. It's not that they just perceive things differently. Events actually turn out differently.

This is more than just the "water glass" idea. You know, some see the water glass as half full and to others it's half empty. If you think about it, this itself is sort of a cynical concept —the idea that things aren't actually different, we just perceive them differently.

What I'm talking about is actually making things different because of one's outlook.

If life begins within the mind, then all success begins within the mind.

The decision to be great, the decision to reach for more are all decisions, which if never made, will never occur.

It sounds so simple as to be almost obvious and yet it's so true. How many times have you experienced that by simply changing your mind about something, you were able to solve some problem, something which seemed unsolvable suddenly seemed simple. (If you haven't experienced this, try it. Try looking at a problem from a different viewpoint and the solution will probably pop right up.)

Some would say that one's past determines one's future. Some would say that one's genes will determine his fate. Yet the actual fact of the matter is that those who believe that they can accomplish big things do, and those who believe that their path is fixed by factors they can't control become fixed by those factors.

So don't fall into the trap of thinking that life is set up

against one to make you fail. Stay positive. Every situation has a solution as long as you believe there is one and never stop looking for it.

So many people think back on their past and wish for better days. They think back to their school days and think fondly that these were the best years of their lives. I hope that when you look back on your time with us to look back fondly as the beginning of many, many great times.

And when someone asks whether you see the water glass as half full or half empty, I want for you to ask: "Do you have anything better than water to drink around this place?" (Not sure this last line is funny or necessary.)

The world needs the next generation of geniuses to move things forward, to correct the mistakes of the present, and for you to provide for your children a world to live in that's better than the one that was given you.

4. The Key to Genius

How do you get the most out of what you have? I'm not referring to only physical things, but also your abilities?

One could save like mad, stockpile things away, bury their valuables in their backyard. Some people seem to feel pretty good about knowing they've got some experience or knowledge under their belts from a good education. One might even get pleasure and take comfort in knowing they're really good at something.

But is it enough to just know you've got a diamond locked away in a safe, or just knowing you have the potential to do something? Maybe. It could likely bring some joy and comfort to your life knowing that one has a lot of potential sitting in the wings, if ever it's needed.

But here's a good question to ask: Is it fun and exciting to think about playing a game, or would there be greater fun and excitement in actually playing a game; maybe even inventing a better game to play?

You might be knowledgeable about things and know you're capable of doing certain things. You might even have some really cool material things. But how do you get the most out of what you know and have, and of which you are capable?

Potential is a funny thing. There is infinite possibility, but nothing really comes of it unless you turn possibility, or even probability, into action.

A bag of seeds are but a bag of round, little kernels. But go out and plant, fertilize and water them, and you can yield a whole lot more, just from those little seeds. A small bag can become acreage of valuable sustenance. Just the same, having a bright mind, having capabilities and knowledge sitting stagnant in your mind, if you don't use that potential to create the greater yield it can make, you will miss out on what life is all about.

None of us should fall short of our true potential. That would be a travesty, like almost popping a bag of popcorn or half-baking a cake and never being able to eat all of the yumminess that awaits. We all have certain gifts, it's up to us to use them.

COMMENCEMENT ADDRESS 4

You are about to enter a different world. Some people call it "the real world." Others say you're about to enter "the jungle." Well that is nonsense. You already live in the real world and anybody who's been to high school knows it's more likely that you're leaving the jungle rather than entering it. I mean it can really seem like a jungle sometimes with tigers, lions and a whole lot of monkeys. I think that parents sometimes make up these scary stories about the "real world" to get you to stay home longer. I know if you were all my children I would.

In actual fact though, some things are going to change for

you and some things are going to remain the same. For example, tomorrow morning you will no longer have to wake up early enough to be late for roll call. On the other hand, you'll still need to listen to your parents (well, at least as much as you do now).

So what is happening tonight? What does it mean to graduate?

Well, it means different things for each one of you. For one thing, this is the ending of the time when you were lucky enough to spend a lot of your days together. Some of you are going off for further studies. Some of you will be entering the workforce and starting your careers. Honestly, I hope it's only one or the other—either more education or work. I mean, I hope you didn't go through all this study just to sit around and play video games. (OK, maybe just a few days of video games.)

You've each taken a different path to get to this point. And from this point on you'll be heading out on your own unique futures.

As much as possible, we try to prepare every student for the accomplishment of his or her own goals. This can be very different from student to student, and as you've seen tonight, all of these graduates have reached the end product of "a student who knows what he wants to do in life and is prepared to get there."

This aligns with my personal belief that every one of our students is a genius in one way or another.

In fact, I even wanted to make a marketing campaign out of that idea, but we scratched it as the word "genius" meant too many different things to different people.

So, what does it mean to be a genius? Normally, if you think someone is genius, it means they're really smart or at least smart at something. But it seems like it should mean something more than just being smart; I'm not really sure.

If only there were some kind of book or something that helped teach one what words meant...

(Open a dictionary)

Per this dictionary ... a genius is ... oh. very interesting ...

You see, the original meaning of the word genius meant "a guardian spirit associated with a person or place." It then came to mean "a spirit that accompanied one from birth" and then "one's natural born abilities and tendencies." The idea being that the spirit that accompanied one from birth influenced a person's abilities and character.

A more modern definition means: "a person who is exceptionally intelligent or creative, either generally or in some particular area."

That's the definition we normally use.

I have a disagreement with this definition though, and since I'm the boss, and as I have the microphone, I think I will take the liberty to add to this definition. And no, my students, you do not have this privilege when doing exams.

You see, just having natural ability doesn't make someone a genius in my book. One actually has to use his talents and intelligence to truly be a genius. Imagine if Einstein never published his theories on advanced physics. He still would have been the smartest man around if he never published his ideas. It's just that no one would know it. He'd still be sitting in a Swiss patent office today. Well, maybe not today, but you get my point. Would anybody have considered him a genius?

Or imagine this...

Imagine if the best writer who ever lived never wrote a word. The world would have been denied his genius. Shakespeare would still have been the best writer in terms of potential, but no one would have known it. I wonder how many geniuses there are out there who are actually only "potential geniuses." Potential because they never took the risks or had the courage to apply their talents fully.

It's interesting to note, too, that the word "genie" has the same root as the word genius. This is probably because what a genius can accomplish sometimes looks like magic to the rest of us.

This definition, in the dictionary, says a genius is "a person who is exceptionally intelligent or creative." It's interesting that creativity is considered a component of genius. Do you see the link-up of intelligence, creativity and then action? To me, real genius includes action.

Each of you have been given a special opportunity because you have parents smart enough and caring enough to ensure you got a great education. Unfortunately, with special opportunity comes special responsibility, or something like that. The world needs the next generation of geniuses to move things forward, to correct the mistakes of the present, and for you to provide for your children a world to live in that's better than the one that was given you.

Please show your appreciation to us and your parents by going out into the world and accomplishing the great things I know you're capable of.

So you see, what we are trying to do in our school is create geniuses. Not just fill your heads with data. Exceptionally smart students who have that spark of creativity and the ability to actually produce those results in life. That is our product.

And when I look at this graduating class, I believe we have accomplished this with each one of you.

Thank You.

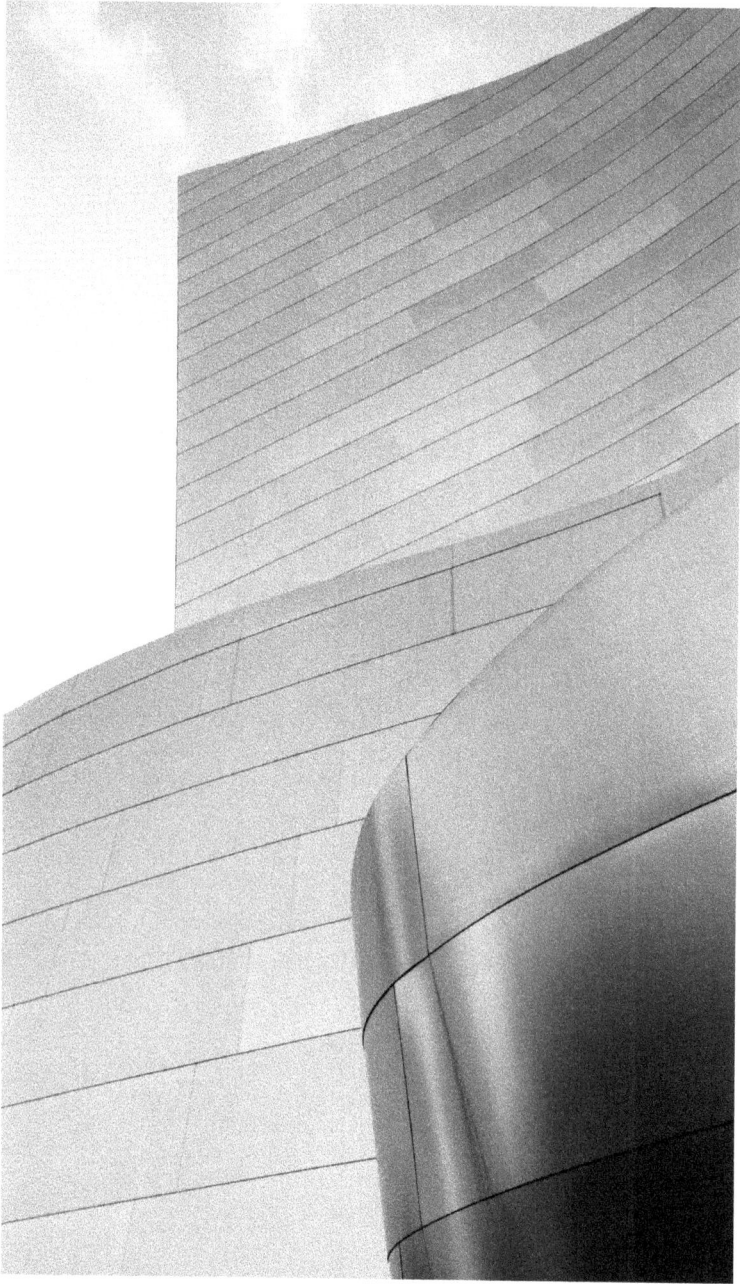

My advice to you on this is that you create your dreams and goals in a pure state without letting all the reasons for failure enter into the equation.

5. On Mediocrity, Greatness, Dreams and Courage

COMMENTARY

In chasing success we often focus on the dream or the vision and sometimes forget the practical realities of what it takes to make those dreams a reality.

Other times people are so locked into reality of life and circumstances that they see no hope for change or greatness.

It really takes both, and there is a way to be a successful and practical dreamer, which I cover in detail in this speech.

BEAR STORY

One of my favorite stories goes like this:

Two men were hiking in the woods. As they were going along, they noticed about a half-mile away there was a bear.

They tried to walk quietly so the bear wouldn't notice

them, but they had these big clunky hiking boots on and they tended to sort of tramp around and make a lot of noise. Additionally, these boots, although good for hiking, slowed the men down a lot.

Sure enough, the bear noticed them and looked up from what he was doing. It was springtime and the bear had just come out of hibernation and was hungry. He was now looking at two big men walking through the forest who would be great for lunch.

The men started to run and the bear started running after them. The men were running as fast as they could but were slowed down with all the gear and boots. So they threw off their gear and ran a little faster, but the bear was still gaining on them. Then one of the men suddenly stopped running, sat down and proceeded to take off his boots. His buddy looked at him like he was crazy and said, "what are you doing? Just taking off your boots won't help you outrun the bear."

The guy looked up and said, "I know, but I don't have to outrun the bear. I only have to outrun you!"

MEDIOCRITY

You see, he didn't need to solve the problem of the bear. He only needed to solve the problem of the bear by being slightly better than his friend.

And although I love this story, it indicates sort of a mentality of mediocrity. According to the "Mr. Zwers Dictionary," Mediocrity means: "only medium quality; not very good." It's like one doesn't need to be truly great or fast or strong, just a bit better or faster or stronger than his or her competition, no matter how poor the competition is.

In many ways and many times in life, this is true—one doesn't have to be the best one could be, just good enough to beat the competition.

This feels good. We all do it. We pride ourselves in being better than someone else. It feels good to know that at least you're not in last place, that you at least beat one other person in the race. But is that really the level one should strive for?

I used to travel a lot. In fact I've been to over 40 countries around the world. And one trait I found common to every country was that every country was certain they were better in some way than some other country.

For example the Australians are superior to the New Zealanders, the Austrians feel superior to the Germans, and the Italians know they're superior to everyone. The only exception to this I found was the U.S. who usually doesn't realize there are any other countries out there.

In other words, judging yourself by how well others are doing around you doesn't lead to a very high standard in life. You can always find someone worse off to compare yourself to. Sometimes it's like three criminals sitting in jail arguing which one is the most ethical. Or three kids on the playground arguing which one is cheating the least. Or three homeless guys arguing whose shopping cart has the best wheels.

The truth is that much of society isn't really built around raising the standards higher, but more about lowering them so people will feel good about themselves. You see this in schools or work places sometimes where a hard-working person is told to slow down because he's making everyone else look bad. It's actually this kind of thinking that has led partially to the recent economic crisis. A lot of greedy people kept pushing the standards of ethics further and further down until the economic system just couldn't bear the load any longer. It was okay, "because everyone else was doing it." This created an economic crisis but that was preceded first by a moral crisis.

So, am I suggesting that you compare yourself to people who are better than you? Well ... no. First of all, because that's demoralizing, and secondly, not everyone can be like me.

My point is actually that you need to set your own high standards and judge things in that context. It's like when our coaches push each young man and woman to be his or her best, not just a little better than the other players.

THOUGHT VERSUS FEELINGS

You see, the point isn't whether one has pride or confidence. The point is, we all do things to make ourselves feel good, feel better about ourselves. After all, sometimes having a high goal or standard can be uncomfortable.

We live in a society where feeling good and feeling good about ourselves has become a national obsession. Feeling good should really be the reward for doing good. When one has accomplished a great task, like tonight's graduates, they should feel good. They have something to be proud of. However, when one's life becomes focused constantly on how he feels, like, "is he bored, is he happy?" instead of "what is he doing, what has he accomplished?" then "feeling good" can just be a distraction, like a drug to take one's attention off of what really matters.

I read a lot of history. It's sort of a hobby of mine. One historian I read pointed out that, in the old times, men were men of action. Their literature and daily lives revolved around what they did. Later on, men became men of thought. What they thought and what they wrote was what mattered. Great thinkers came out this time.

Great thinkers and great doers built this great nation in which we live. It seems to me, however, in the last 50 years or so, we've become a nation of feelings. The motto has become: "If it feels good, do it." Decisions are being made based on how people feel. Politics is based almost entirely on people's feelings. Television is flooded with advertising for drugs, alcohol and other diversions intended to manipulate or distract people's feelings.

The only concern I have about this is that I believe feelings and emotions are there as a reward for having taken the correct actions in one's life. And when this reward system gets short-circuited, and we become more and more soft and distracted, there will be less and less "doers" in society to carry the load of the "feelers."

There's a difference between feeling good and doing good. This is part of the importance of what we are trying to accomplish as a school: building a nation of doers again.

GREATNESS

So, the standard I want for each of our graduates tonight is a standard of greatness—top level—envisioning and reaching for the top in everything you do, whatever that means for each of you personally.

DREAMS

The best route to greatness I know of is actually through one's dreams and one's decisions. Not all dreams and decisions are successful, but one hundred percent of non-decisions definitely end in failure, guaranteed. So, production is important, but so are dreams. And it's important that you all take time to dream, and dream big.

And by dreaming, I don't mean just daydreaming; not dreaming in the passive sense, but dreaming in an active sense, postulating, intending, and planning. These are ways dreams can manifest themselves in the physical world.

It takes courage to dream big. To start out on a path that you know failure is possible on, but the potential rewards are great. It's much more comfortable to take the safe path, the certain road. But the rewards along that path are few. It takes courage to dream big, knowing that others might laugh at you, laugh at your dreams, telling you that "you won't make it" or that "your dreams are stupid." It takes courage to overcome one's own doubts and uncertainties, to go forth into the jungle of life.

DREAMS, THEN COURAGE

Courage isn't the absence of fear but continuing on in spite of your fears.

Often when trying to accomplish something great or

large, one thinks of all the reasons it can't be done or why it won't work, so why should one try at all? My advice to you on this is that you create your dreams and goals in a pure state without letting all the reasons for failure enter into the equation. Then, with that goal clearly in mind, deal with all the reasons for possible failure. Not the other way around. Thinking of all the barriers first and then creating a goal that fits in nicely in the little box that the barriers have created for you just results in small goals.

To accomplish greatness requires work and dedication. It means spending more time working than playing, being more of a producer than a consumer. Now, here is a life secret for you...

The cost of greatness is really the same cost as mediocrity: Upsets, problems and sleepless nights. You'll get them both whether you are trying to accomplish greatness or avoid greatness. It's just that the problems are better problems and the rewards are much, much better when you reach for great goals.

Wrap-up

So, you can work hard to not work, or work hard to accomplish great things. Either way, you're going to be working hard; again, one of them just has better rewards.

No one knows what tomorrow will bring, so we try to prepare you as best we can. This might seem like I'm putting a lot of pressure on you. Yeah, I am, but only because I have confidence in your abilities and power. And with great power comes great movie lines. Besides, that big bear coming down the hill is going to put pressure on you anyway. So I'd rather you felt the pressure of your own goals than someone else's.

So, enjoy tonight (you've earned it), and make tomorrow great. Set your goals high—and then go accomplish them. And if you ever need help, let us know. We'll be here for you.

Anyway, the future we are preparing you for isn't one that's predetermined or set in stone but one that you will create and build for yourselves and for your children and grandchildren. It is up to you to make it a bright future.

6. Luck and the Future

Commentary

There are two perspectives one can take with life. One is that things are the way they are, nothing can be done about it, things were meant to be this way. The other has an outlook on life that's the complete opposite: one where we ourselves influence the way things are and will be.

The first perspective might appear to be the easy way: a free ride on the shoulders of someone or something else that has control. One might even think there are no other options and that things are predetermined and unchangeable. The hand that has been dealt is the way it is.

But having no say in the way you should live your life is no easy ride, and definitely not a pleasurable journey. Having no say only allows for complaints about how poorly things are being run. It can't allow for much happiness and satisfaction. It's a pretty grim way to go through life, if you ask me.

The second perspective comes with an eraser, an easel, paint brushes and a full array of paints—in oil or acrylic, the choice is yours.

You don't like the way something is? You have the understanding that you have limitless choices and, from there, can come up with great ideas and plans in how you're going to make it better.

This second perspective offers vision, the ability to live in the moment while designing the future for yourself. Wow! How much more exciting is that?

Having a say in life only requires that you look out each day and realize that you are the artist and the world is your canvas. It's your canvas and you have a limitless amount of paint.

COMMENCEMENT ADDRESS 5

As graduates, you have your whole lives ahead of you. And as you journey down the road of life, I wish you happiness and "good luck."

LUCK

But what is luck?

The Roman philosopher, Seneca, said that luck is what happens "when preparation meets opportunity." "When preparation meets opportunity …"

This is different than gambling luck which is when your money becomes someone else's opportunity.

And that's what we, as a school, are doing—preparing you, preparing you for life, preparing you for the future. And we've tried to do so to the best of our ability.

The real question becomes, "What are we preparing you for exactly?"

Some of you are prepared for college, some of you directly

for work; minimally I hope you are prepared for getting prepared.

There are things we do as a school to help prepare you.

Our education is a combination of liberal arts as well as practical subjects. Liberal arts include things like literature, philosophy and history. And it's these things which give the practical subjects, like math and sciences, value and importance. Otherwise, we'd just be creating hollow, materialistic individuals.

That's why we try to balance both the cultural and the practical. So, when you wonder why you have to read history or literature when they aren't related to your future professions, it's because we don't only want you to graduate a good producer, but also a good person.

PREPARATION AND THE FUTURE

But, ultimately, when we're talking about preparation, we're talking about preparing for the future. What about the future? Isn't this supposed to be the future? And where is my flying car I was promised? I mean, it is the 21st century already.

But what is the future? What do we mean when we talk about it? Should we be trying to guess what it holds and try to predict it? Are we trying to get on the right path now, to meet it like a train meeting us at some future station?

I like to think of it in terms described by the scholar and political theorist, John Scharr: "The future is not the result of choices among alternative paths offered by the present, but a place that is created—created first in the mind and will, created next in activity. The future is not some place we are going to, but one we are creating. The paths are not to be found, but made, and the activity of making them changes both the maker and the destination."

Let me repeat that: "The future is not the result of choices among alternative paths offered by the present, but a place that is created—created first in the mind and will, created next in activity. The future is not some place we are going to, but one we are creating. The paths are not to be found, but made, and the activity of making them changes both the maker and the destination."

So again, it's not a matter of finding and following the right path as much as it is envisioning and creating the future you want. Not following a path but creating one. And that is what we aim to prepare you for.

Society is unstable and constantly changing and no one knows what the future holds. Our responsibility and mission is to get you as prepared as possible.

OPPORTUNITY

So, luck consists of "preparation meeting opportunity." We talked about preparation; now let's talk about opportunity. We've worked to prepare you. It's up to you to seek out the opportunities.

Again, the key is to be prepared for opportunities when they arrive; you don't always get to choose when an opportunity arises, and if you're not prepared, an opportunity can look like a problem rather than an opportunity.

For example, Megan Fox's date bails on her for the Academy Awards. She asks you to go instead (opportunity), but because you don't have a nice suit to wear, you have a problem and have to say "no." Preparation would have turned this problem into opportunity.

ADVENTURE AND RISK

Part of seeking out opportunities is having a sense of adventure — to boldly take on life without letting your fears hold you back.

Like our old friend the Roman philosopher Seneca says: "It is not because things are difficult that we do not dare, it is because we do not dare that they are difficult."

Because societies seem to be designed in such a way that the ideal citizen is quiet, works hard, and pays his taxes, anything beyond that is often made to look scary or dangerous. Therefore, as American society grows larger, it also becomes more controlling and more intolerant of action.

As an example of this, I think of how things have changed since I was young and it reminds me of a story that was in the local news a few years ago.

A couple of kids about 12 years old hopped the fence at their school and found that one of the school buses on the property had the keys left in the ignition. So the boys started up the bus and drove around the parking lot for a while until someone caught them. The news report mentioned that security footage showed the boys were laughing while committing this "terrible crime."

And although I agree that the kids probably should have

gotten in trouble for this mischief, they actually got arrested instead. When I was growing up, this would've been a call to my father, not a call to the police (which actually might've been worse than getting arrested). But the fact that this is viewed as a crime nowadays rather than childhood misbehavior is scary. Now these kids are in the system, have a record, and no doubt have been put under some sort of therapy as to why they thought it was funny to drive a school bus around the property.

Again, more rules and restrictions are being placed on our actions and I'd like to remind the future generation in this room that these restrictions are made by men to restrict men and can also be eliminated by freedom-loving people to set men free.

My point is that I believe that life can be fun and I hope that the haters don't eliminate all fun and joy from life in the name of political correctness or fear.

So I hope that as the future generations in this room grow up, you do not become timid but instead relish life and seek out greater and greater opportunities.

A great piece of advice on this from former First Lady, Eleanor Roosevelt, is: "Do one thing every day that scares you."

Anyway, the future we are preparing you for isn't one that's predetermined or set in stone but one that you will create and build for yourselves and for your children and grandchildren. It is up to you to make it a bright future.

Lastly, I originally wished you luck and happiness. Neither of these are a goal in themselves but are the byproduct of doing the right things, making the right decisions and living well. In this way, we can achieve true happiness. Stay thirsty, my friends.

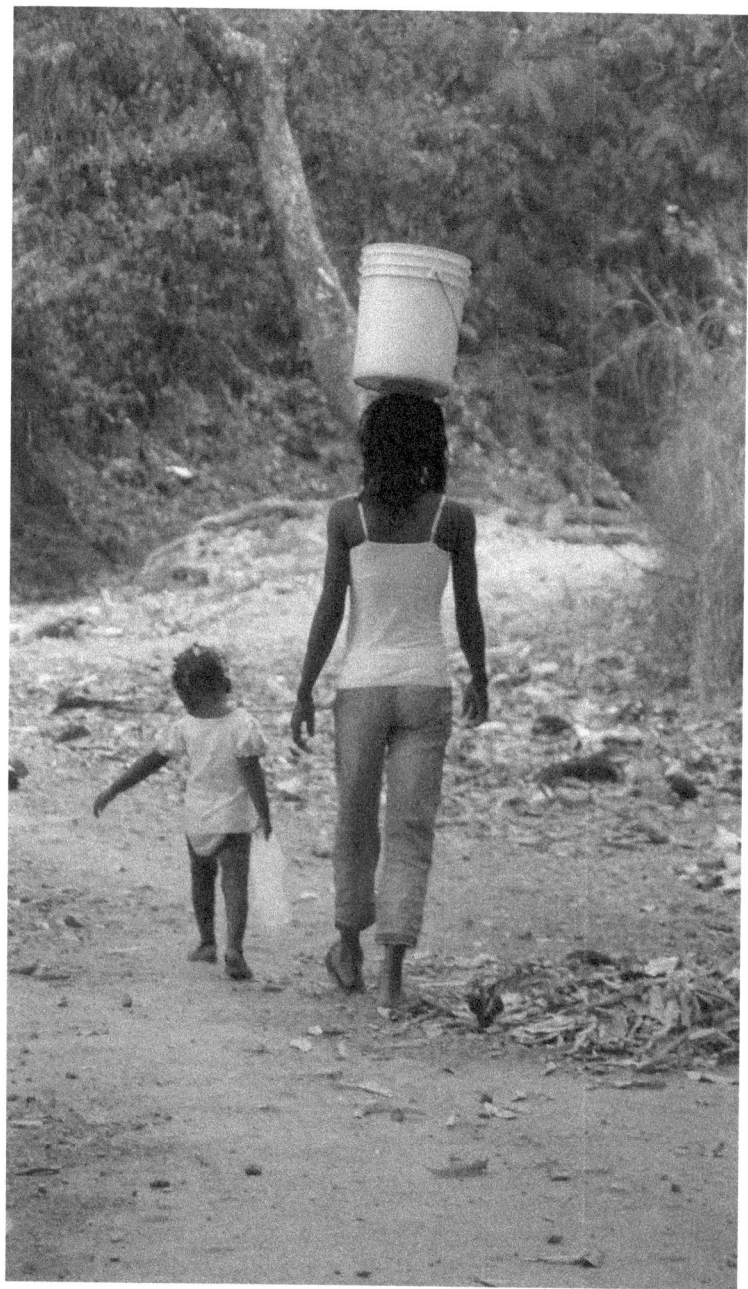

If you have clear beliefs and stick to them, you are as strong as a fortress. Strength is not about fighting but about being unmovable when challenged.

7. FIVE GIFTS FROM MY MOTHER

COMMENTARY

Our experiences influence us in who we choose to be, how we live our lives. It's all about choices. It's amazing to think that by decision alone, we can change the course we're on, just as much as change our hairstyle.

This is why it's a very good idea to only allow great individuals to be in your immediate environment, your life. Because sooner or later, wittingly or unwittingly, you will be influenced by those around you, especially those in close vicinity.

An example of this is when a child decides to never ever be like his mother or father ... or whomever. But no matter how hard he insists on that, he, later in life, hears himself saying the words, "I'm just like my mother, father or whomever."

As a nature of being human, we tend to emulate others, pick up their mannerisms, even their behaviors and reasoning. This human trait—good, bad or indifferent—makes being around people, whom you respect and admire, pretty important.

For instance, hanging around people who aspire to be "successful," but their motive is to cheat the system by avoiding work and robbing banks, would not be people you would want to associate with. Eventually, they will be robbing you.

On the positive side of this, there are great individuals you know now, and will come to know, who are supportive of your goals and have a good head on their shoulders, too. There's no reason to become them or copy them, but to simply share the similarity of goals, intentions and purposes, and help one another and benefit from each other. You will experience less conflict, and much of the opposition you do face will be for your best interest, whether you realize it or not at the time.

This graduation was one where my daughter was graduating and my mother was coming out for the ceremony. My mother had never heard me speak live before, so I wanted to surprise her with a speech themed around her. Needless to say, she was very surprised and happy.

COMMENCEMENT ADDRESS 6

INTRO

In the stock market there is a term called Alpha. It stands for the amount one is making or losing, relative to the market as a whole. For example, if the stock market is up by 10% but your investments are only up by 5%, you're not doing a very good job because basically, if you did nothing (theoretically) you'd have made 10%. The 10% is like a free gift.

On the other side, if the market is down 10% and you're only down 5% you've done better.

In terms of life, I think that this concept has a lot to do with fulfilling one's potential. Sticking with financial examples, if you grew up in a nice society, had a good upbringing and education, but as an adult you lived in a small, dirty apartment, drove a piece-of-junk car and were a burden to everyone around you, you'd be less than living up to your potential.

If, however, you grew up on the streets of a poor country, homeless and hungry, you'd be exceeding from where you started out, and your Alpha rating would be high. You would actually be closer to achieving your potential than the first example.

By potential I mean "being and accomplishing the most you are capable of," not just cruising along at a safe and comfortable level, but going beyond what is comfortable to achieve all you can in life.

It means taking the things you've been given, your talents, your education, your opportunities and making the most out of them and the most out of yourself.

Making the most out of ourselves and our lives is something we should all have as a goal, maximizing our value to ourselves and others.

They used to say, "He who dies with the most toys wins."

Actually, he who most reaches his potential is the winner regardless of how many toys he has.

We've all been given opportunities, things, knowledge. What we do with them is what determines if we are successful. It's what determines our value as people. How much do you use of what you've been given? How much have you expanded that even more and improved yourself and the world around you?

I've recently become aware of certain beliefs and values I have that make me who I am.

Thinking specifically about certain values I have and where I first got them from, I realized that much of these came from my mother. These are like gifts from her. Tonight, I want to talk about five gifts in particular.

Hopefully, I can relay these to you and thereby regift them for your use, too.

I didn't really realize until recently that my mom was such a great influence in my life. She helped establish what I believe in, what my values are. The rest has just been finding out how to accomplish them.

Gift 1: Knowing the Difference Between "Need" and "Want"

Being a single parent of seven children, my mom had to raise us the best she could, with very limited resources. That's a euphemism for "we were poor—really poor."

As a result, we learned early on the difference between the words "need" and "want." You "need" food, you "want" a toy. Not that we didn't have food, it's just an example. And as for toys, you can always make your own out of sticks or whatever.

But the lesson I learned from this was that money isn't everything. You don't need money to be happy.

If you think you do, stop whining. It's just an excuse.

It's like Eleanor Roosevelt said: "Happiness is not a goal ... it's a by-product of a life well-lived."

Now, this doesn't mean you shouldn't work hard and try to become rich, but it does mean doing things just to get money will not lead to happiness. We were one of the poorest families I knew growing up, but we were also the happiest.

I remember one of the best Christmases I ever had was the year I got a stick and rock for a present. No, I'm just kidding. It was the 1970s, not 1770s. And, I didn't grow up in the Great Depression like my mother did.

The main point here is that I've had the benefit of growing up and knowing what was important and what was just nice to have. And the advantage of that is you get to enjoy both the needed things and the wanted things more when you know which is which.

GIFT 2: STRENGTH

My mother always demonstrated a moral strength and high principles. As a child, it always seemed to me that she was rock solid on what was right and what was wrong. And she wouldn't waver when she'd made up her mind about something.

You have to understand that my mother was not someone you would think was particularly strong if you met her, but she had an inner strength and that was what I learned. If you have clear beliefs and stick to them, you are as strong as a fortress. Strength is not about fighting but about being unmovable when challenged.

I like to say: "You don't get to choose when you go to war."

I say that to my staff sometimes when some emergency comes up at the worst possible time (which emergencies always do). By this I mean, when it's time to go to war it's time to go to war, and wishing the war would go away until another time is pointless.

For example, when you have children of your own, you'll discover your children will need you. And when they need you, you have to be there for them and it probably won't be on your schedule.

My mother had the strength of her generation—those individuals who lived through the Great Depression and World War II—and she knew that when it was time to go to war, it was time to go to war.

She demonstrated this courage when she had to kick out my dad who was a toxic element in our household (another euphemism).

Forcing my father to leave the house knowing she'd have to raise seven kids on her own. This was an example of the bravery and integrity she had. It was a thing she did to protect the sanity of herself and the family.

You don't get to choose when you go to war, but you'd best be prepared for it when it comes.

GIFT 3: A POSITIVE ATTITUDE

She always maintains an upbeat, positive attitude. And that applied to us as well; there was a "No Whining" policy in our house.

Whining was seen as an inability to handle things on your own, weakness.

With my mom, the glass is always full (at least 50% water 50% air = 100% = Full).

Part of that positiveness was the insistence that we try new things and have new adventures.

Like when I was eleven years old, and she sent my fourteen-year-old sister and me across country by Greyhound bus. I mean, can you imagine doing that today? It'd be considered child abuse today. But at that time, it was a great adventure, and I've loved going to new places and exploring new cultures ever since. If you ever want to explore a different culture, take the bus cross-country.

Part of that positiveness had a practical side, too. It included telling us that, "If we didn't have anything good to say about a person, then say nothing at all." If she didn't have anything to say about a person, we all knew what that meant. She taught us that we should love everyone but we didn't have to trust them.

Gift 4: A Sense of Fun

My mother has a great sense of humor, and I'm sure that she's the funniest person she knows.

In our house, even when things were bad, there was always a sense that things would be okay and that it was okay to have fun and to be funny.

She used to quote, "God has a sense of humor, just look at a giraffe."

I learned that humor is an essential element of life, not

just a luxury for good times.

She always found lots to do that was interesting, fun and cheap. She made up for a lack of money with creativity.

She never said this, but I feel I learned from her example that life becomes a lot more fun when you don't care what anyone thinks of you. I could give a whole speech just on this one point. It's like Oscar Wilde said, "Be yourself; everyone else is already taken."

GIFT 5: MAGIC IS EVERYWHERE

Growing up, our home was a magical place because it was a creative place filled with adventures.

It was a place that, in one year alone, was visited by the Easter Bunny, Santa, and a little elf who watched if we were being good or bad and maybe even a guardian angel or two.

I love the fact that I grew up in a house where anything seemed possible.

It's like the quote by Albert Einstein, "There are only two ways to live your life. One is as though nothing is a miracle. The other is as though everything is a miracle."

The final piece of magic from her was a feeling that I will always be loved. It is amazing, the security and confidence something like that can give a person.

CLOSING

Now, I'm sure that I've misquoted my mother in some of this, and there is much, much more I learned from her, like to always hold the door open for others. And I'm sure this doesn't sum up her entire personality, but these are the things that I remember and how I remember them.

I'm also not saying that I am entirely who I am because of my mother, but I did choose to accept certain values and beliefs from her, and these have helped me come closer to reaching my potential. These are the gifts and opportunities I have been given and I have to live up to, just as you have received much and now have the responsibility to live up to that and to begin the quest to reach your potential.

Finally, this isn't only my mom's story but just my version of many moms' stories. And, looking back, it's sometimes important to get a historical perspective on where we are and how we got here. Sometimes we don't have to look that far back in history, just a generation or two.

There are so many times where we want to do what is safe, easy, and comfortable. But this doesn't force us to grow, become better, to learn and to truly reach our potential.

8. Choices

We hear about life as being a journey. As with just about everything, there seems to be conflicting data; "It's about the journey" or "It's about getting to the finish line."

I think we run into somewhat opposite ideas because there are usually multiple truths within the general aspect of what is being said.

Finding the truth in things is the key to succeeding, because truth is what allows us to move toward and achieve our goals.

So, are life's paths about the journey or reaching the desired end point? There is truth in both of them. The journeys we decide to take can be pleasurable or unpleasant, productive or fruitless, in any combination. But life is about wins and losses, successes and not so much success. It's experiencing life.

So we have choices that we make (and change at any time we want to) and hopefully we can actually enjoy the journey.

The destination can be glorious, especially out of a lot of hard work and struggle. The sense of accomplishment against all odds can be fantastic. But it can also be the end of the game, so the pleasure can be short sometimes.

Making the best of your life by first living it to the fullest will automatically place you on many paths and finish lines. The most important thing is to be willing to go out and experience both the journey and the destination, whatever it may be.

Commencement Address 8

Intro

Goals are an important thing in life. They give us direction and something to strive for.

People without goals are less likely to be successful and accomplish much less, so it's important to have them. In fact, success is often measured almost solely by how effective one is in accomplishing his or her goals.

Paths

Some modern-day philosophers say that it is about the journey, not the destination. Sometimes I wonder if this is just said to make people feel better about failing, or if some people really just wander around "journeying" with no destination in mind.

I mean, when you're going to Disney World, you're not going like, "Oh boy! Can't wait for that car ride. It's going to be awesome!"

This brings to mind a story I heard once about a European

settler of some country, speaking to one of the local population who was just sitting under a tree. The European man looked down at the man and asked him why he was just sitting around.

And the guy replied, "What else should I be doing?"

And the European said, "Well, working."

"Why?"

"So you can make money."

"Why do I need that?"

"So you can buy all the stuff you need and then retire and take it easy."

"We'll, I'm doing that now."

You see, both men had the same goal, to take it easy but two very different ways of getting there.

So maybe the path you take to your goal does matter.

Choosing Paths

Picking a path is like picking a profession or a purpose. There are often many ways to accomplish the same goal. You could accomplish fame equally by robbing a bank or by curing some disease, and, in fact, now-a-days, you're probably more likely to become famous from some such notorious act.

The problem with the subject of paths is in picking the right one. Is it better to take the shortcut that leads straight through the dark forest of Mirkwood or take the much longer and surer path around the forest?

This is tricky because, although one path might seem better than another, there is always a chance that a path is a false path that doesn't take you to your goals at all.

There is a Chinese proverb which says, "If you keep doing what you're doing, you're likely to get to where you're going."

What does this mean? It means that every action you are doing is on a path taking you somewhere, and you are 100% guaranteed to arrive at the end of that path (good or bad) as long as you stay on that path.

So, it does matter what path we choose. Choosing and following a path is the one way we have of controlling our destiny. 90% OF LIFE IS JOURNEY.

Picking the right path is important. For one thing, you don't want to pick a path that doesn't get you to your goals. Secondly, you don't want a path that has you doing something you hate, even if it does take you to your desired goal.

It's interesting to think that 93.6% of our lives is spent in trying to achieve our goals and only a small amount actually enjoying having our goals. I used to think that it was 90% but when you add in sleep and take out holidays, obviously the number is 93.6%.

For example, climbing Mount Everest takes months of preparation and climbing. But once you're up there, it's like, "Yep, I'm pretty high up now. Nice view. Time to climb down, I guess."

Another example is what makes NFL quarterback Peyton Manning so successful: he likes PREPARING for games nearly as much as playing them. He likes the path to success as much as the success itself.

The best description of this comes from Bobby Knight, one of the most successful college basketball coaches of all time. When talking about college recruits, he said, "Don't give me a player who likes to win. Give me a player who likes to prepare to win." Everybody likes to win, not everybody likes the work and effort involved in preparing to be a winner. It's a lot harder.

As an example from my own experience, I used to be a professional photographer—a dream job for many people, and it was for me, too. I specialized in studio photography and used to set up these elaborate sets for my shoots. In fact, after spending time selling to clients, running the business side of the studio, and building sets, I really probably only spent about 5% of my time as a photographer. But fortunately I liked the other stuff, too, so it wasn't a problem. If I hadn't, I think I would have been very unhappy.

Hard Work

This is where the topic of hard work comes in. A lot of times, the path we know we should be on requires hard work; very rarely is just having talent or being lucky enough to make it. We're always told that the key to success is hard work. Parents say it, we say it at school, society says it. Is it true? Does hard work guarantee success? I don't know if it does, but I can pretty much guarantee laziness leads to failure.

But actually, what do we think of when we say "hard work"? We've all had times when we were working hard and loving it, and other times not. A recent Internet survey asked people to define hard work, and 90% of the people said that "hard work" was "doing work you don't enjoy."

So if you love what you are doing, then it doesn't feel like "hard work." It might be difficult, and it might be challenging, but most of us don't have a problem with this.

So, in choosing the right path, picking the easiest path shouldn't be as important as picking a path we enjoy.

TAKING RISKS

Part of pursuing a path means you need to take risks. Hard work alone won't make you a success; you are going to have to take some risks at some point. It starts with picking a path.

Life is like a quest; you set out after the Holy Grail, fight some monsters, and maybe rescue a princess or two along the way.

If your life doesn't seem like this, then maybe it's because you're watching an online version of someone else's life.

This is called risk/rewards: if you never take any risks, you'll wind up denying yourself some awesome rewards.

When my wife was a young girl growing up in Switzerland, she spent winters up in the Alps. Imagine little Kathy in her little dress and pigtails running around up there.

Well, when she was done milking the cows, feeding the goats, and making the chocolate for the day, she was allowed to spend the rest of the day skiing.

One day, when she came back from a particularly good day of skiing, she boasted to her Uncle Adrian that she skied the whole afternoon without falling down once. Uncle Adrian was a very good athlete and expert skier himself, so little Kathy was certain that he'd be extremely proud of her. Well, you can imagine her surprise when Uncle Adrian frowned at her and said that he wasn't impressed at all, and if she didn't fall at all, it merely meant that she didn't push herself, and if she didn't push herself, she'd never really become a good skier.

This is a true story (mostly true except for the cows and goats, although she did actually make chocolate). But Uncle Adrian really said this to Kathy, and it's advice that is as true today as it was when he said that twenty years ago ... when my wife was seven years old.

Uncle Adrian was right, and his advice applies to you and your lives as much as it did to little Kathy all those years ago.

You see, there are so many times where we want to do what is safe, easy and comfortable. But this doesn't force us to grow, become better, to learn and to truly reach our potential.

SUCCESS VS. FULFILLMENT

Coming back to the idea of the journey vs. the destination, you see there are two rewards with which we get to measure our success. The final reward, be that a lot of money, a big house, etc., and the reward we experience every day—a feeling of fulfillment we get from knowing we are progressing on the right path.

Following your dreams and doing good things gives you a sense of fulfillment; accomplishing your goals gives you a feeling of success.

BALANCE

So the best is to have a balance of both: good goals and the right path to accomplish them.

This is the best way to bring balance to the Force. By the way, did you ever notice that the Jedi always tried to bring "balance" by killing off all their enemies? Wouldn't balance be 50/50?

Anyway, in your lives, I recommend finding out what you love to do, and then figure out how to make it pay.

CLOSING

So, where are you going in life? Where will you end up? Life is a funny thing sometimes, and you don't always end up where you think you will. Most people still don't believe I'm a school principal.

You just need to set out to go somewhere and be prepared for the adventure that is life. We've done our best to prepare you, the rest is up to you.

Thank you.

The point is that the best insurance for the future is to be prepared for anything and be up for everything.

9. THE FUTURE

COMMENTARY

There is so much bad news and threatening information constantly hitting us that it can sometimes seem that there is no hope for the future. I strongly disagree and especially disagree when young people are given a hopeless and negative outlook concerning the world around them.

In this speech, I really wanted to stress the opportunities the future holds if one is willing to reach for them.

COMMENCEMENT ADDRESS 9

PREDICTIONS

Right now, you have completed one phase of your lives and are about to head out into the rest of it. And like a young tiger who was raised in captivity and then released into the wild, your first steps out into the world will be cautious and uncertain. Where are you going? How will you make it? And what should you do? These are all questions you probably have about the future, and honestly, today and every day, everyone in this room is heading out together into the great unknown future.

Prediction of the future is something we all would like to be able to do, something that if we could do, would make all our lives so much better (and so much more boring).

There are those, like stock brokers, whose jobs are to predict the future, and many self-proclaimed prophets who claim to know what will happen next.

Like Charles H. Duell who famously claimed, "Everything that can be invented has been invented," which would have been fine, except Mr. Duell was head of the US Patent Office, and the time this was said was 1899. Ah, old-timey people, they were so dumb.

I'm sure now-a-days we have a much better idea of the future. I remember that when I was your age, killer bees were to have taken over and killed America, and of course, flying cars. At least I can finally make a call on my watch.

So, actually, I'm not sure that we do have a better grasp of the future than Mr. Duell did.

THE IMPORTANCE OF LEARNING

In fact, I could talk about my ideas of the future all night, and I'd probably be wrong on most of them (well, some of them.)

But the truth is that the future is a constantly moving target, and no prediction will ever be 100% right (other than I predict that Knights Football will go undefeated again this year.)

The point is that the best insurance for the future is to be prepared for anything and be up for everything.

The best way to be prepared for anything is to be able to

learn anything. If one can learn anything, then he can do anything.

The key in this is that, although your high school days are over, you should always be trying to learn and better yourself, or for short: ABL = Always Be Learning. As long as you're learning, you'll never be bored.

Learning is Everywhere

We learn from books and teachers, but we also learn from life.

What do you get out of experiences? What do we learn from our mistakes? A smart man learns from his mistakes. A wise man learns from the mistakes of others.

So listen, watch and learn. Become a sponge for knowledge and understanding. Learning is everywhere when we look with wonder and curiosity. As long as you stay curious, you'll stay young. I hope you all stay curious and experience the joy of life-long learning.

Part of learning from life requires taking risks and taking on challenges. Sometimes there is a cost to adventure, but sometimes there is also a cost to not taking an adventure. Like an old saying from India, "Only kings who go into battle fall off their horses." Being safe and cautious also means you won't get the rewards and glory of accomplishing something great.

IMPORTANCE OF BEING PREPARED FOR THE FUTURE

To take on the world, you are going to need resources, and your mind is your greatest asset.

In fact, the human mind is a resource that mustn't be wasted, must be developed. It must be cared for and sharpened like a knife.

Mankind and all our futures depend on having a large amount of smart people. Therefore, it's actually our social obligation to be prepared, to be as educated and able as we can be.

Man is not insignificant in the universe. And (MIBs aside) as far as we know, we may be the only force in the universe that is capable of changing it. We have the power to change the world. Our lack of reason and understanding is our only barrier.

CONCLUSION - THE FUTURE LOOKS BRIGHT FOR THOSE WHO SEIZE IT

Despite Mr. Duell's prediction, so many great advancements have been made in the last century: the growth and spread of civil rights, the curing of diseases, the technologies that give a single person the ability to reach millions.

As a final quote, I'd like to correct my mis-quoting of Mr. Duell earlier. See, although he is attributed with the earlier prediction of the future, he never actually said that.

In fact, Mr. Duell said in 1902, "In my opinion, all previous advances in the various lines of invention will appear totally insignificant when compared with those which the present century will witness. I almost wish that I might live my life over again to see the wonders which are at the threshold."

Plot twist!

And that, my friends, is why I am extremely jealous of you: not because of what you'll be able to experience, but for what you'll be able to create, because the world you live in is going to be more interesting and surprising than anything my generation could imagine.

The question remains, "Is the future bright or bleak?" That depends on you. My prediction is that it's going to be amazing.

CONCLUSION

Hopefully this book has been of some value and given you some inspiration and motivation to reach out and accomplish more. Minimally, you should have some new perspectives on how to look at things.

We all face many decisions in life, and in these pages are some of the best ways I know of to reach the best conclusions. You may be facing some life decisions right now, or maybe not. In any case, I hope that you will keep this book and refer to it again when you need to.

I believe that everyone's goal is to make as many right decisions as he or she can. If we remain tough and not make too many bad decisions, we can hopefully get to where we want to be in life.

And that is my hope for you, reader, that you are able to reach out and fulfill your potential and accomplish your dreams.

About the Author

Jim Zwers has traveled around the world to over forty countries and spoken on education in China and around the United States. One of his passions is lecturing to parents and educators.

Since 2002, Jim has been the Executive Director of Clearwater Academy International. From this position, he has been able to establish, maintain, and forward important reforms in education that have helped to unlock the greatest potential in students. This is something of which he is most proud.

During this time span as Executive Director, Mr. Zwers also helped open a school in Haiti.

He plans to continue to expand Clearwater Academy International while helping other students and educators fulfill their commendable missions.

www.ingramcontent.com/pod-product-compliance
Lightning Source LLC
Chambersburg PA
CBHW060953040426
42445CB00011B/1143